Diseases and Disabilities Caused by Weight Problems:
The Overloaded Body

Obesity: Modern-Day Epidemic

Diseases and Disabilities Caused by Weight Problems:
The Overloaded Body

by
Jean Ford

Mason Crest Publishers
Philadelphia

First printing
1 2 3 4 5 6 7 8 9 10
Library of Congress Cataloging-in-Publication Data

Ford, Jean.
  Diseases and disabilities caused by weight problems : the overloaded body / by Jean Ford.
     p. cm. — (Obesity: modern-day epidemic)
  ISBN 1-59084-944-2—ISBN 1-59084-941-8 (series)
 1. Obesity—Complications—Juvenile literature. I. Title. II. Obesity (Philadelphia, Pa.)
 RC628.F67 2005
 616.3'98—dc22

                                    2004026240

Produced by Harding House Publishing Service, Inc., Vestal, New York.
Cover design by Michelle Bouch.
Interior design by Michelle Bouch and MK Bassett-Harvey.
Printed in the Hashemite Kingdom of Jordan.

Contents

Introduction

We as a society often reserve our harshest criticism for those conditions we understand the least. Such is the case with obesity. Obesity is a chronic and often-fatal disease that accounts for 400,000 deaths each year. It is second only to smoking as a cause of premature death in the United States. People suffering from obesity need understanding, support, and medical assistance. Yet what they often receive is scorn.

Today, children are the fastest growing segment of the obese population in the United States. This constitutes a public health crisis of enormous proportions. Living with childhood obesity affects self-esteem, employment, and attainment of higher education. But childhood obesity is much more than a social stigma. It has serious health consequences.

Childhood obesity increases the risk for poor health in adulthood and premature death. Depression, diabetes, asthma, gallstones, orthopedic diseases, and other obesity-related conditions are all on the rise in children. Recent estimates suggest that 30 to 50 percent of children born in 2000 will develop type 2 diabetes mellitus—a leading cause of preventable blindness, kidney failure, heart disease, stroke, and amputations. Obesity is undoubtedly the most pressing nutritional disorder among young people today.

This series is an excellent first step toward understanding the obesity crisis and profiling approaches for remedying it. If we are to reverse obesity's current trend, there must be family, community, and national objectives promoting healthy eating and exercise. As a nation, we must demand broad-based public-health initiatives to limit TV watching, curtail junk food advertising toward children, and promote physical activity. More than rhetoric, these need to be our rallying cry. Anything short of this will eventually fail, and within our lifetime obesity will become the leading cause of death in the United States if not in the world.

Victor F. Garcia, M.D.
Founder, Bariatric Surgery Center
Cincinnati Children's Hospital Medical Center
Professor of Pediatrics and Surgery
School of Medicine
University of Cincinnati

Chapter 1

Weighing In: Defining the Problem

- The Epidemic
- The Definition
- What's the Problem?

Was there really a time when people *wanted* to be chubby? Remarkably, yes! At the turn of the nineteenth century, when the leading causes of death were tuberculosis, pneumonia, and diarrheal diseases, most people desired fuller figures. Plumpness was "in." Society equated a bulbous belly with robust health, not to mention wealth.

Why? One reason is that many health professionals believed a little extra fat helped people withstand the ravages of disease. The medical community even recommended weight gain for those "cursed" with skinny frames (today we would call those people "blessed") and provided instructions for cultivating extra fat. Consider these words by two turn-of-the-century physicians:

Persons who desire to become plump and remain so should retire about 9 or 10 P.M., and sleep until 6 or 7 A.M. . . . The breakfast should be plain and substantial. . . . A course of fresh ripe fruit should first be eaten, then potatoes, meat or fried mush, or oatmeal porridge, bread and butter. The drink may be cocoa or milk-and-water, sweetened. . . . The hearty meal of the day should not come later than five hours after breakfast. About 3 or 4 P.M. a drink of water should be taken. Supper should be light; bread-and-butter and tea, with some mild sauce. . . . Another method of becoming plump is a free diet of oysters. . . . To sum up, then: to become plump, one must use plenty of water, starchy foods, oysters, fats, vegetables, sweets, and take plenty of rest. By following the instructions, lean or spare persons will become fleshy or plump. (Drs. George P. Wood and E. H. Ruddock, *Vitalogy or Encyclopedia of Health and Home,* 1901).

Today, these doctors' words are fascinating, even humorous, but our weight problem is not. Overweight and obesity have reached epidemic proportions in the United States. Working in a world rife with poverty and disease, these doctors never could have foreseen that someday it would be not only too easy for most Americans to gain weight, but almost impossible for many of them to lose weight. That obesity-related ailments would replace all infectious diseases as killers of Americans would have seemed impossible. These doctors surely could not have guessed the dire effects America's fattening would have on individuals and on society at large. If only they knew of the impending health crisis.

The Epidemic

Weight-related issues and obesity are a serious and growing health problem in America. According to an article in the *Washington Post*, the average American adult put on eight pounds between 1980 and 1991. That trend continued through the nineties. "In 1990, about fifty-six percent of adult Americans were overweight, and twenty-three percent were obese," cites the American College of Physicians' *Annals of Internal Medicine*. "By 2000, sixty-four percent were overweight and thirty-one percent were obese." Fifty-six percent up to 64 percent and 23 percent up to 31 percent in just one decade? Those are dramatic increases.

The National Institutes of Health (NIH) and the National Institute of Diabetes and Digestive and Kidney Diseases (NIDDK) substantiate these figures. According to the 1999–2000 National Health and Nutrition Examination Survey (NHANES), over two-thirds of U.S. adults are overweight, and nearly one-third are obese.

So overweight and obesity are clearly concerns for our nation's adults, but what about young people? The statistics are similarly alarming. One study appearing in the January 2004 issue of the *Archives of Pediatrics and Adolescent Medicine* reports that U.S. teens are far more likely to be overweight than teens from fifteen other industrialized nations. In the study, researchers tabulated the body mass indexes (BMIs) of 29,242 teens, ages thirteen to fifteen, from Austria, the Czech Republic, Denmark, Finland, Flemish Belgium, France, Germany, Greece, Ireland, Israel, Lithuania, Portugal, Slovakia, Sweden, and the United States. The results should concern most Americans.

According to the study, U.S. children were the most likely to be overweight. Among thirteen-year-old students, 10.8 percent of U.S. girls and 12.6 percent of U.S. boys were overweight. Among fifteen-year-olds, the percentage rose: 15.1 percent of U.S. girls and 13.9 percent of U.S. boys. That's more than one in ten for both ages.

Compare those figures with the next-highest proportion of overweight thirteen- and fifteen-year-old girls (Portugal at 8.3 and 6.7 percent, respectively) and the next-highest proportion of overweight thirteen- and fifteen-year-old boys (Greece at 8.9 and 10.8 percent, respectively). Most strikingly, compare U.S. statistics with Lithuania's. Its *greatest* incidence of overweight teens is only about one in fifty! If overweight adolescents have an increased likelihood of being overweight or obese in adulthood (which they do), and if overweight and obese adults are at increased risk for serious health issues like heart disease and diabetes (which they are), future America is in big trouble!

 # The Definition

Clearly, the problem of our growing waistlines has become widespread, but what do these terms "overweight" and "obese" really mean? Although these words are sensitive topics that can quickly cause hurt feelings and offense, both expressions are used here strictly as medical classifications. They are merely terms the health-care community assigns to specific height-to-weight ratios—nothing more.

Generally speaking, the term "overweight" refers to excess body *weight* (not necessarily *fat*) compared to medically set standards for height. The excess can come from muscle, bone, fat, and/or water. "Obesity" specifically refers to having an abnormally high amount of excess body *fat* (also known as adipose tissue). Technically, the terms are distinct from one another, although many people mistakenly use them interchangeably. A person can be overweight and not obese. Obese persons, however, are always overweight.

Health experts use a number of methods to determine if someone is overweight or obese. For example, you may be surprised to learn that the most accurate method for calculating body fat is by submerging a person in water. This is also known as hydrostatic weighing. Think about getting into a bathtub. Before you step into the tub, the water is at one level. As you lower your body into the tub, the water level rises. The difference between the water level before you enter and the water level after is the amount of water your body has displaced. During a hydrostatic weigh-in, a doctor or technician measures the amount of water displaced by a patient's body and then uses a mathematical formula to translate that displacement into an extremely accurate estimate of body fat percentage. Few medical facilities, however, have the equipment and personnel to offer hydrostatic weighing, so it's rarely used. Most people must rely on slightly less accurate, but more *accessible* means of estimating their body fat percentage.

Worldwide Waistlines

Two agencies of the U.S. Department of Health and Human Services, as well as institutions in fifteen other countries, collected survey information in 1997 and 1998 to gauge overweight and obesity rates of teens worldwide. The results of the study appear in the January 2004 issue of the *Archives of Pediatrics and Adolescent Medicines*. We've listed the top three contenders and the country with the lowest proportion of overweight children below.

WORLDWIDE WAISTLINES				
Rank	Country	Age	Gender	Percentage Overweight
1	United States	13	Girls	10.80
2	Portugal	13	Girls	8.30
3	Ireland	13	Girls	6.60
15	Lithuania	13	Girls	2.60
1	United States	15	Girls	15.10
2	Portugal	15	Girls	67.00
3	Denmark	15	Girls	6.50
15	Lithuania	15	Girls	2.10
1	United States	13	Boys	12.6
2	Greece	13	Boys	8.9
3	Ireland	13	Boys	7.0
15	Lithuania	13	Boys	1.8
1	United States	15	Boys	13.9
2	Greece	15	Boys	10.8
3	Israel	15	Boys	6.8
15	Lithuania	15	Boys	.08

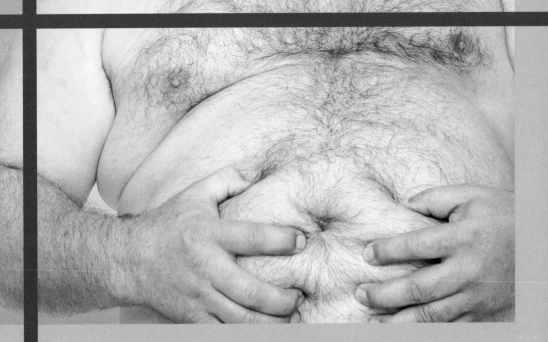

One of the common techniques for determining how much body fat a person has is by "pinching an inch" with a device called a caliper. A caliper measures skin-fold thickness at various locations on the body (underarm, waist, hip, thigh, etc.). These measurements are used to estimate the total amount of fat in a person's body. Although caliper measurements are easy to take, calculating one's body fat with this method still requires the help of a medical professional, fitness expert, or someone else who has the measurement tools and knows how to use them properly. For this reason, the most common and easiest tool used today for estimating body fat is something called BMI.

What is BMI, and how do we calculate it? BMI is a formula that uses a person's height and weight to estimate the percentage of his body that is made up of adipose tissue. BMI is less accurate than hydrostatic weighing or caliper measurements, but according to the NIH, for most people BMI is still a reliable indicator of approximate body fat, the defining element of obesity. To calculate your BMI, divide your weight in pounds by your height in inches squared, then multiply by 704.5. (The NIH uses the multiplier 704.5, but other organizations use slightly different multipliers such as 703 or 700. The variation in outcome, usually just a few tenths of a point, is insignificant for most people.) Or, for metric measurements, divide your weight in kilograms by your height in meters squared. The two formulas look like this:

[Weight in pounds ÷ (height in inches x height in inches)] x 704.5 = BMI

[Weight in kilograms ÷ (height in meters x height in meters)] x 704.5 = BMI

Once you have your result, compare it to this chart to determine whether your amount of body fat falls into a healthy range.

BMI	CLASSIFICATION
< 18.5	= Underweight
18.5–24.9	= Normal
25.0–29.9	= Overweight
30.0 and above	= Obese

(Source: U.S. Centers for Disease Control and Prevention [CDC])

Here is a sample formula for a person who is five-feet, three-inches tall (63 inches) and weighs 120 pounds (Notice we are using the U.S. rather than the metric formula):

[120 ÷ (63 x 63)] x 704.5 = BMI
[120 ÷ (3969)] x 704.5 = BMI
[.03] x 704.5 = 21.14

The person in our example has a BMI of 21 and thus falls within the normal range.

Keep in mind that BMI ranges are simply practical *guides* for defining overweight and obesity. They are not rigid cutoff points. In fact, overweight

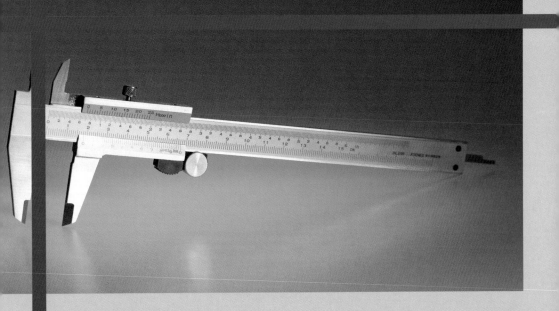

and obesity classifications have proven difficult to pin down. The NIH describes obesity as "an excess of body fat frequently resulting in significant impairment of health," but the exact point at which such impairment occurs is not precise and differs from person to person. The United States Public Health Service concedes this fact: "An ideal, health-oriented definition of obesity would be based on the degree of excess body fat at which health risks to individuals begin to increase. No such definition exists."

Because precise definitions for overweight and obesity are elusive and different people will suffer health impairments at different levels of weight, tools like BMI are just the start of the *diagnostic* process. Doctors also consider symptoms like breathlessness, fatigue, blood pressure, resting heart rate, swelling in the legs, accumulations of body fat noted via the "eyeball test" (that is, their observational skills), and other factors when determining whether a person is a healthy or unhealthy weight.

To understand the limitations of BMI alone as a diagnostic tool for determining healthy body size, think about the following two cases:

Andrew is five-feet, five-inches tall and weighs 155 pounds. He's the star of the swim team, sporting muscular shoulders, upper arms, and thighs. To look at him, you'd think he didn't have an ounce of body fat.

His trim physique is toned and firm, and his cardiovascular endurance is unbelievable; he can swim 500 meters with ease.

Jonathan is the class geek and proud of it. He scored 1450 on the SATs, and he's a computer genius who spends hours at his keyboard. At five feet, seven inches and 155 pounds, he's slim but couldn't run a mile if his life depended on it. Just going upstairs to math class leaves him winded! The word exercise is definitely not in his vocabulary, and his body shows it; his abdomen is soft and wrinkly, and his thighs, thin as they are, jiggle.

One day Andrew and Jonathan calculate their BMIs as part of a health project. Jonathan's is 24 (in the "normal" range), but Andrew's BMI is 28 (in the overweight range). If people looked solely at these numbers to determine these boys' health, they'd say Jonathan was in better physical condition than Andrew. But he's not. How can this be?

Andrew and Jonathan illustrate an important lesson about BMI: It is not the sole indicator of health. It is just one of many indicators, including diet, physical activity, waist circumference, blood pressure, cholesterol levels, family history, and blood sugar. Because muscle tissue is much heavier than fat tissue, BMI often overestimates body fat in muscle builders and other athletes. This is what has happened to Andrew in our example. In fact, according to BMI alone, Arnold Schwarzenegger, Sylvester Stallone, and Jean-Claude Van Damme are all "obese." On the other hand, the index can underestimate body fat in the elderly and others who have lost muscle mass. Lastly, BMI offers no means of measuring heart-healthiness such as blood pressure or cholesterol levels. BMI is merely one tool most effectively applied in conjunction with other diagnostic measurements.

Despite its limitations, BMI is the most commonly used method for determining if someone is overweight or obese. It is the measurement of choice for many health professionals. The NIH, the CDC, the National Heart, Lung and Blood Institute (NHLBI), the NIDDK, and the World Health Organization all concur that a BMI of 25 to 29.9 defines overweight, and a BMI over 30 indicates obesity. Although not a direct measure of percentage of body fat, BMI is a more accurate indicator of the character of body mass than weight alone.

What's the Problem?

So why should we care if American adults and teens are getting fatter? Why should we concern ourselves with things like overweight or obesity? The answer is simple: The health risks of overweight and obesity are too serious to ignore. Excess fat impairs the function of many body systems and organs, leading to multiple health issues and even death. Two-thirds of us will face those issues down the road, and if we don't, we definitely know someone who will. But how can we know how much risk we face?

Doctors can predict likely health problems based on the degree of being overweight and the location of fatty deposits in a person's body. For example, a person whose fat is located primarily in the abdominal region is at greater risk of heart disease, hypertension, and diabetes than the person whose fatty-tissue deposits are concentrated in the buttocks and thighs.

U.S. Government Recommended Weights for Men and Women

Height	Weight (Age 19-34)	Weight (Age 35+)
5'0"	97–28 lbs	108–138 lbs
5'1"	101–132 lbs	111–143 lbs
5'2"	104–137 lbs	115–148 lbs
5'3"	107–141 lbs	119–152 lbs
5'4"	111–146 lbs	122–157 lbs
5'5"	114–150 lbs	126–162 lbs
5'6"	118–155 lbs	130–167 lbs
5'7"	121–160 lbs	134–172 lbs
5'8"	125–164 lbs	138–178 lbs
5'9"	129–169 lbs	142–183 lbs
5'10"	132–174 lbs	146–188 lbs
5'11"	136–179 lbs	151–194 lbs
6'0"	140–184 lbs	155–199 lbs
6'1"	144–189 lbs	159–205 lbs
6'2"	148–195 lbs	164–210 lbs

(Source: U.S. Department of Health and Human Services)

Classes of Obesity by Degree of Overweight

Classification	Men (% of Ideal Weight: BMI)	Women (% of Ideal Weight: BMI)
Ideal Body Weight	100%: 22	100%: 21
Overweight	110%: 25–29.9	120%: 25–29.9
Obese	135%: 30–34.9	145%: 30–34.9
Significant Obesity	160%: 35–44.9	170%: 35–44.9
Morbid Obesity	200%: 45–49.9	220%: 45–49.9
Super Obesity	225%: >50	245%: >50

(Source: "Morbid Obesity: Weighing the Treatment Options," *Nutrition Today*)

Based on such patterns, researchers have further defined BMI guidelines and types of obesity. Doctors recommend weight ranges considered ideal for certain heights and then combine these ideal weights with factors like BMI and *anatomical* distribution of fat to better assess a patient's risk of developing obesity-related illnesses.

Once a person has had his or her excess weight evaluated by a health professional, he or she can begin exploring options for addressing the weight issue. What will happen if people don't act to address their weight issues? What exactly is at stake? Consider the words of humorist Robert Orben: "Quit worrying about your health. It'll go away." Although he meant the statement to be funny, this writer and editor penned perhaps no truer words. If we choose to ignore our health, it will go away. We must pay attention to our growing waistlines and act if need be. (Every height has a recommended weight range for a reason!)

Prevalence of Medical Conditions by Body Mass Index

(Prevalence is indicated as percentages of that population.)

Medical Condition	BMI 18.5–24.9	BMI 25–29.9	BMI 30–34.9	BMI >40
Diabetes (men)	2.03%	4.93%	10.10%	10.65%
Diabetes (women)	2.38%	7.12%	7.24%	19.89%
Heart Disease (men)	8.84%	9.60%	16.01%	13.95%
Heart Disease (women)	6.87%	11.13%	12.56%	19.22%
High Blood Pressure (men)	23.47%	34.16%	48.95%	64.53%
High Blood Pressure (women)	23.26%	38.77%	47.95%	63.16%
Osteoarthritis (men)	2.59%	4.55%	4.66%	10.04%
Osteoarthritis (women)	5.22%	8.53%	9.94%	17.19%

(Source: U.S. Health and Nutrition Examination Survey)

Types of Obesity by Anatomical Distribution of Fat

According to the *American Journal of Clinical Nutrition,* the following are the four types of obesity based on location of fatty deposits on the body.

TYPE I: Excess BMI or fat percentage; no particular concentration in any one area.

TYPE II: Excess subcutaneous fat on the trunk, particularly the abdominal region (also called android or male-type obesity).

TYPE III: Excess fat in the abdominal visceral area.

TYPE IV: Excess fat in the buttocks and thighs (also called gynoid or female-type obesity).

In addition to the obvious practical and social difficulties excess weight can bring, it also increases one's risk of developing serious illnesses. What are these illnesses? Diabetes, heart disease, and some forms of cancer are all associated with obesity and can be fatal. Additional conditions like osteoarthritis, sleep disorders, psychological impairments, and reproductive issues are also common problems associated with obesity. These conditions, although not life threatening, can significantly interfere with one's quality of life and become real challenges for those affected.

Chapter 2

Not So Sweet: Diabetes

- Type 2 Diabetes
- Complications of Diabetes
- Symptoms
- Where Do We Go from Here?

Tara's mother has five sisters. She and two of these sisters are overweight. Tara's grandmother is also overweight. One day, Tara overhears her mother talking with her doctor.

"Well, *two* of my sisters developed diabetes in their fifties. . . . Yes, Mom has it, too . . . uh huh . . . I see. . . . Will I need insulin?"

The lightbulb goes off in Tara's mind: her mom has diabetes. *I don't get it,* she puzzles. *I thought you were born with diabetes, but Mom never had it before.* After a moment Tara begins to worry. *Will Mom be okay? Can I get it, too?*

There are three main kinds of diabetes: type 1 diabetes (also called juvenile diabetes), type 2 diabetes (previously called adult-onset), and gestational diabetes. All forms of diabetes are related to the way blood-sugar levels (the amount of sugar that is in your bloodstream at any given time) are regulated by insulin (the hormone responsible for getting sugar out of the bloodstream and into your cells). The different forms of diabetes, however, have different causes. Type 1 diabetes is an *autoimmune* disorder in which a person's immune system (the system responsible for killing viruses, bacteria, and diseased cells) attacks and destroys the beta cells in the pancreas (the organ where insulin is made). With the beta cells destroyed, the pancreas can no longer produce insulin, and the person with diabetes must give himself regular insulin shots to regulate his blood-sugar level. Type 1 diabetes is a very serious disease requiring constant medical management, but it's relatively rare.

Gestational diabetes is a complication that can occur during pregnancy. Certain hormones produced during pregnancy can interfere with insulin function and production, and diabetes can result. Although gestational diabetes can be serious, once the pregnancy is over, the patient's blood-sugar and insulin levels usually return to normal. Neither gestational nor type 1 diabetes is caused by obesity (although obesity could worsen the condition). Only type 2 diabetes is directly associated with overweight and obesity. This is the type of diabetes Tara's mother has developed.

Type 2 Diabetes

In the past, doctors referred to type 2 diabetes as adult-onset diabetes because it occurred almost exclusively in adults. In adulthood, people tend to become less active and gain weight, especially during one's forties, fifties, sixties, and beyond. However, the medical community now refers to adult-onset diabetes as type 2 diabetes (or noninsulin-dependent diabetes mellitus, NIDDM) because as childhood obesity has increased over recent decades, so too has the number of diabetic children. Doctors now understand that type 2 diabetes develops at any age, even in childhood, suggesting that age is not as strong an influence on the condition as obesity is. The term "adult" simply no longer applies to this disease. Today, 90 to 95 percent of all diabetes cases are type 2.

So what exactly is type 2 diabetes? When a person has this condition, his

body makes too little insulin (this is called insulin deficiency) or doesn't properly use the insulin it does make (this is called insulin resistance). As many as 92 percent of people with type 2 diabetes are insulin resistant, so we'll focus here. What does "insulin resistant" mean?

When we eat carbohydrates (foods such as cereal, fruit, starchy vegetables, pasta, rice, bread, cookies, or muffins), our bodies convert the food into blood sugar (glucose) to give us the energy we need to maintain life. Our blood carries this glucose to all the cells in our body (fat, muscle, and organ cells). Insulin, produced by beta cells in the pancreas, is the hormone that lets that glucose into our cells. Insulin acts much like a key, unlocking cells to let in the glucose.

Once glucose enters a cell, that cell has three options for how to use it: it can immediately use the glucose for energy; it can store the glucose form called glycogen for use in the near future; or it can convert the glucose into fat for long-term energy storage. As cells take in the glucose, overall glucose levels in the blood drop, signaling the pancreas to stop making insulin. (Otherwise cells would keep letting in more blood sugar and deplete blood-glucose levels to an unhealthy low, a condition called hypoglycemia.)

Myth-Busters

Many people mistakenly believe that the following factors cause type 2 diabetes. They do not!

Sugar: Eating excessive quantities of sugar alone does not cause diabetes. If eating excessive sugar, however, contributes to a person becoming overweight or obese, then in that way it can play a role in the development of the disease. (Excessive amounts of protein or fat will do the same thing.)

Gender: Males and females are equally likely to develop diabetes.

Emotions: Changes in emotions do not trigger type 2 diabetes.

Stress: Stress does not cause diabetes, but, like sugar, stress can contribute to weight gain. If you eat more to manage your stress and then gain weight, the excess weight—not stress—may influence the disease's development.

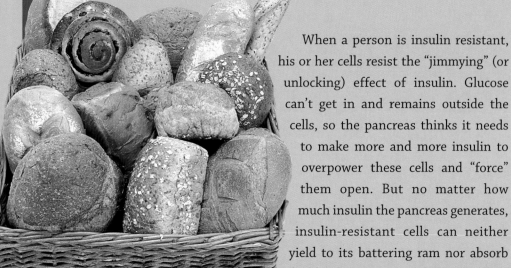

When a person is insulin resistant, his or her cells resist the "jimmying" (or unlocking) effect of insulin. Glucose can't get in and remains outside the cells, so the pancreas thinks it needs to make more and more insulin to overpower these cells and "force" them open. But no matter how much insulin the pancreas generates, insulin-resistant cells can neither yield to its battering ram nor absorb the blood sugar waiting behind it. Cells remain impenetrable, and glucose stays in the blood, elevating blood-sugar levels.

Since glucose can't get into the cells, the cells run out of energy. Furthermore, the pancreas soon wears out from *chronic* overproduction and eventually loses its ability to produce enough insulin. At that point, glucose remains in the blood, locked out of cells unused, and blood-sugar levels get higher and higher. That's not good. According to the NIH, a high blood-sugar level is a major cause of heart disease, kidney disease, *stroke*, blindness, and early death.

Some cases of type 2 diabetes are preventable. Why? This type of diabetes is almost always associated with excess weight. In fact, obesity influences the prevalence of type 2 diabetes more often than any other factor. According to the American Obesity Association (AOA), fully 90 percent of those with type 2 diabetes are overweight or obese. Anyone with a BMI over twenty-five is at risk of developing this disease.

How does surplus weight trigger the disease's onset? No one knows for sure, but some theories exist. One idea is that being overweight or obese causes cells to change, making them insulin resistant. (We already know that as we gain weight, fat cells change by expanding. Could other cells also change with regard to insulin response?)

Another theory points to adipose (fatty) tissue hiding deep within your central torso, near your organs. This is also called *visceral* fat. You might have heard some people refer to such fat as their "spare tire." Measuring this "waistline fat" is another means of assessing risk. Why? Visceral fat churns out more by-products than other fat cells, including free fatty acids. Researchers think these acids and other by-products harmfully affect surrounding cells and organs—they're sort of like garbage polluting your body's environment. Could they also cause insulin resistance? Some scientists suspect so, but at the moment they just don't know for sure. According to the NIH, however, one's risk of developing type 2 diabetes (as well as heart disease) increases substantially for men with a waist measurement over forty inches and for women with a waist measurement over thirty-five inches.

Whatever the *physiological* mechanism, we do know that excess weight kicks type 2 diabetes into action. As is the case with other forms of diabetes, *genetics* probably predispose a person to the disease. Unlike the other forms of diabetes, however, environmental factors such as lack of exercise and obesity usually set the disease in motion. Consequently, many cases of type 2 are preventable. Think about the following case:

Lyle and Leslie are *fraternal twins*. At fifteen years old, both stayed active and fit through sports. Both ate as well as their parents could

Facing Facts
Eighty-five percent of all children diagnosed with type 2 diabetes are obese.
(Source: Wellness International Network, Ltd.)

encourage. The twins' BMIs ran routinely in the low 20s, and they never worried about health.

Now Lyle and Leslie are twenty-one-year-olds. The *sedentary* life of writing term papers and studying, combined with cafeteria food and midnight vending-machine raids, caused Leslie to gain the traditional "freshman twenty" during her first year away at college. She never did anything about it. Three years later, at five-feet tall and 155 pounds, her BMI soared to 30.

Lyle didn't gain any weight during his college years. In fact, he chose to live more healthfully while on campus, swimming laps three times a week at the pool and running on the university's track. He was also careful about what and how much he ate and drank. His BMI remained a normal 22.

In her early twenties, Leslie starts to notice that she's always thirsty, plus she has to urinate often. Additionally, she feels fatigued more than she ever has, even during the day. She knows she doesn't get much exercise and that she's gained weight, so she writes off her fatigue to being out of shape. Then her vision starts to blur. Too much time on the computer, she thinks.

Lyle suggests Leslie see her doctor. Type 2 diabetes runs in their family, and Leslie's symptoms are classic. Separate blood tests reveal glucose levels of 220 and 260 milligrams per deciliter (anything over 126 is high). Leslie does indeed have type 2 diabetes.

Why did Leslie develop diabetes and Lyle didn't? After all, they both likely carry the genes for it, not to mention the fact that they're twins. The key lies in lifestyle and fitness choices. Think about it. If a potential diabetic never develops the obesity necessary for jump-starting her genetic disorder, those genes won't be activated, and the disease won't develop. The excess fat simply isn't there to trigger it. So by staying fit, we can prevent this kind of diabetes' onset and literally extend our lives, or at least preserve our quality of life. Each and every one of us should strive to maintain ideal body weight if we want to avoid type 2 diabetes.

Why would we want to avoid this disease? Is it really that bad?

Glucose Guidelines

The National Institute of Diabetes suggests the following guidelines for maintaining healthy blood-sugar levels:

When	Ideal or Targeted Blood-Glucose Levels
Before meals	90 to 125 milligrams per deciliter
One to two hours after the start of a meal	less than 160 milligrams per deciliter

Complications of Diabetes

If one develops type 2 diabetes, he or she becomes vulnerable to a host of other long-term medical issues. According to the Mayo Clinic, male diabetics are twice as likely to develop coronary artery disease as men who do not have diabetes; women diabetics are five times as likely as healthy women to develop coronary artery disease. (We will discuss heart diseases at greater length in chapter 3.) Both are five times more likely to encounter hardening of the arteries or have a stroke because of circulation-related issues.

Decreased circulation is a very common side effect of diabetes and has a negative impact on all parts of the body. For example, circulation problems can impact internal organs like the kidneys. Chronic high blood-sugar levels eventually cause blood vessels in the kidneys to block or leak, resulting in impaired ability to filter waste from the blood. Harmful waste products then remain in the blood and build up, a potentially fatal condition. Forty-three percent of serious kidney disease—that which requires *dialysis*—is diabetes related. But damage to blood vessels is not limited to the kidneys. Diabetes can attack blood vessels everywhere, from the nerves in your eyes to the muscles in your feet and legs. Damage to the vessels that supply blood to the eyes leads to diabetic retinopathy (the leading cause of new cases of adult blindness in the United States), glaucoma, and cataracts. Damage to blood vessels in the legs frequently leads to slow-healing ulcers on the feet or lower extremities. Because of blood-vessel damage and related circulatory complications, infection becomes a huge risk.

Over time, diabetes can also cause nerve damage (neuropathy), including paralysis. As many as 70 percent of diabetics have some form of diabetic neuropathy. This condition can affect many parts of the body and limit a person's mobility. Limited mobility can compound overweight and obesity by making exercise difficult or impossible.

Premature death, heart disease, slow-healing and painful wounds, infections, blindness, nerve damage—all are common, eventual outcomes of diabetes. This disease means business! And it's frequently a side effect of being overweight. Especially if diabetes runs in our families, we *must* pay attention to any weight gain and our overall fitness, in addition to other risk factors.

So what are the risk factors for type 2 diabetes? The biggest risk factors are genetics, a BMI over 25, a sedentary lifestyle, and *ethnicity*. The first, genetics, plays a major role in developing diabetes. If one of your parents or siblings has type 2 diabetes, you are at an elevated risk of developing it because you likely carry the genetic predisposition for it. Having grandparents, uncles, and aunts with the disease may also signify that you are at an elevated risk.

The next most important risk factor is your BMI. If your BMI is over 25, you're at greater risk of the disorder kicking in. Yes, diabetes is usually genetic, but fitness level and lifestyle can prevent, postpone, or trigger its onset. This is especially important to remember because even if your family has always carried genes for diabetes susceptibility, if no one within the family has experienced excess weight, those genes may never have been expressed, and you may be completely unaware that a genetic risk exists. If you are the first person in the family to experience a weight problem, you may also be the first person to tap into that genetic predisposition.

Another extremely important influence on one's likelihood for developing type 2 diabetes is lifestyle. Is your lifestyle primarily sedentary? Do you

Ethnicity and Type 2 Diabetes

Population Group	Incidence in that Population
Non-Latino White Population	6.20%
Native Americans/Alaskan Natives	15.10%
African Americans	13.00%
Hispanic/Latino Americans	10.20%

(Source: American Diabetes Association)

get enough regular exercise? Exercise, or lack of exercise, is a major determining factor in obesity and thus in the development of type 2 diabetes. The more inactive a person is, the higher her chance of developing obesity and type 2 diabetes.

The final risk factor you should be aware of is ethnicity. African Americans, Hispanic and Latino Americans, Native Americans, and Asian Americans all have a greater chance of developing type 2 diabetes than non-Hispanic, white Americans. In fact, one study indicated that Native Hawaiians are twice as likely to have diabetes than white residents of Hawaii. Although numerous theories are in development, at this point researchers don't know exactly why certain ethnic groups are at greater risk for developing diabetes than other groups. Some of these theories rest on genetics while others rest on *socioeconomic* and *cultural* issues like the amount and quality of health care certain groups have access to and the types of foods certain groups eat.

Although decreasing in significance as the obesity epidemic rises, an additional risk factor to consider is your age. While type 2 diabetes can develop at any age, once you hit forty-five, your chances of encountering the condition go way up. But again, this increased likelihood of developing the disease is probably due to weight gain from the less-active lifestyles and slowing metabolism that go along with aging. A final risk factor is having given birth to a baby who weighed more than nine pounds or having developed gestational diabetes during a pregnancy. If either applies, a person's chance of getting type 2 diabetes later in life increases by nearly 40 percent.

Symptoms

So now you know many of the factors that put one at risk for diabetes, but how can you tell if you're actually developing the disease? The symptoms for this kind of diabetes usually develop slowly and may go undiagnosed for months or even years. Regular medical checkups can help identify the condition. Some of the most common symptoms that a person can watch for, however, are:

feeling really thirsty frequently
urinating often
being very hungry more often than usual
feeling tired all the time
noticing blurred vision
developing sores that heal slowly
healing slowly (wounds)
sensing "pins and needles" or tingling in feet
having itchy skin, particularly in extremities
frequent vaginal or bladder infections
finding sugar in urine (identified by a urine test)

You may have one or more of these symptoms before you even find out you have diabetes. Or you may have no signs at all. "Pre-diabetes" is a relatively new classification doctors assign to those people who have blood-

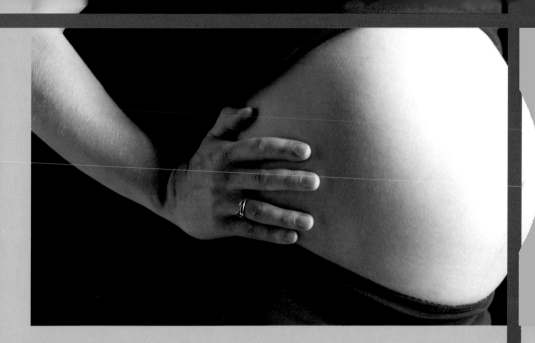

glucose levels higher than normal but not high enough for a diabetes diagnosis (140–199 mg two hours after the beginning of a meal, 100–125 mg after an overnight fast). Their elevated glucose levels indicate some insulin resistance, but these people may not exhibit any additional symptoms.

Obviously pre-diabetics have a much greater risk of developing type 2 diabetes than those with normal blood-sugar levels. Nearly 40 percent of U.S. adults are pre-diabetic, and many will go on to develop type 2 diabetes within ten years.

If a person suspects she has type 2 diabetes, she should see her doctor right away. The recommended screening test for this condition is a blood test called the fasting blood glucose (FBG) or the fasting blood sugar (FBS) test. For this test, the patient must not eat or drink anything (except water) for six hours. Blood is then drawn and the amount of sugar in the blood measured. If the results of your test are equal to or greater than 126 milligrams per deciliter, your physician will likely order a repeat test for a different day. If that test also comes out greater than 126, then you most likely have type 2 diabetes.

Where Do We Go from Here?

If you are at risk for type 2 diabetes, take heart! Lifestyle changes in diet and exercise, plus losing just a little weight, can prevent or delay the onset of the disease. This fact is true for people of all ages and ethnicities.

In a 2002 study conducted by NIH, participants who made lifestyle changes resulting in losing seven percent of their body weight reduced their risk of developing type 2 diabetes by 58 percent! That's only a fourteen-pound loss for a person weighing 200 pounds. Weight loss of as little as five percent reduces high blood-sugar levels, thereby reducing the risk of other health complications. That's only ten pounds for a 200-pound person.

Clearly, management of type 2 diabetes requires weight reduction (to a BMI ≤ 25) and exercise, exercise, exercise! How can these factors impact blood sugar? Exercise helps manage diabetes by lowering blood-sugar levels (when you exercise, more glucose needs to be burned for energy). Exercise and weight loss can also actually reverse insulin resistance, thereby enabling more cells to open up and take in glucose. Even a modest weight loss of eight to ten pounds can help.

Frightening Fact
According to the CDC, every twenty-five seconds someone in America is diagnosed with type 2 diabetes.

Keep in mind that because each person's body and lifestyle are unique, each person's nutritional needs are different. Likewise, each person's ability and commitment to exercise varies, so no single diet or exercise plan can be effective for everyone. You and your doctor should work together to design your individualized health plan to prevent, postpone, or manage type 2 diabetes in your life.

But sometimes diet modifications, weight loss, and exercise are not enough. When they're not, a doctor may also have to prescribe medications that will help stabilize and maintain healthy glucose levels. Some people may feel a sense of failure if they cannot manage diabetes without insulin shots, glucose-lowering medications, or oral medications that decrease insulin resistance. A sense of failure, however, is unwarranted. The goal is to control one's blood-sugar level so that one can become healthier, and for some people that simply requires medication. Preventing or delaying type 2 diabetes and its complications depends on it.

chapter 3

The Silent Killer: High Blood Pressure and Heart Disease

- Coronary Artery Disease

- High Blood Pressure

Fifteen-year-old Becky is getting her physical for summer camp. She's not very concerned, although she knows her doctor will want her to lose weight. Since the onset of puberty, Becky has gotten pretty chubby. She's already clinically overweight and quickly approaching obesity.

Patiently waiting for the doctor to finish taking her blood pressure, Becky becomes concerned when he pauses and then without a word takes her blood pressure again.

"Have you noticed any dizziness recently?" her physician inquires as he finishes the second test.

I wonder what this is all about, Becky puzzles. "No, not really," she replies.

"Well, your blood pressure is pretty high," the doctor continues. "High enough that we need to do something about it."

High blood pressure! Becky can't believe it. *That's for old people!*

Perhaps you, like many people, believe high blood pressure is an adult concern, nothing children or teens need to worry about. If you do, you're dead wrong! Researchers from Tulane University and the NIH's National Heart, Lung and Blood Institute recently released results from a joint survey indicating high blood pressure is on the rise among children and youth. Lifestyle choices and excess fat seem to be the direct causes. Fast-food and junk-food diets, plus hours each day on the computer or in front of the TV equals weight gain in the form of adipose tissue. America's children are getting fat.

Being overweight or obese at any age courts many kinds of cardiovascular disease, not just high blood pressure. The CDC reports that the prevalence of many forms of heart disease among the obese is twice that encountered by individuals of "normal" weight. That's alarming when you consider that one in three Americans is obese, and more than one in two is at least overweight. Even more alarming, the American Heart Association estimates approximately 300,000 people in the United States alone die of weight-related heart issues each year, making obesity the second most prevalent preventable cause of death.

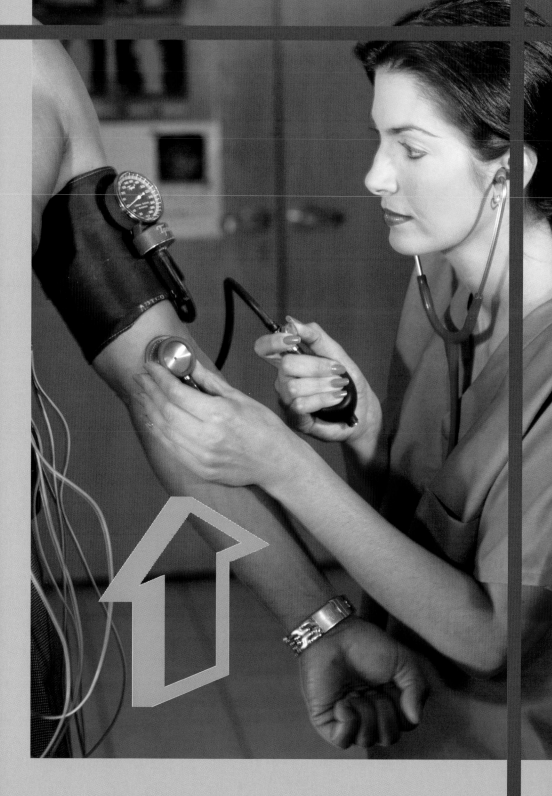

Exactly how does excess fat cause cardiovascular disease? One way has to do with structural changes that occur in the heart as a person gains weight. Your heart has four chambers. The lower-left chamber is called the left ventricle, and it pumps oxygen-enriched blood out of the heart to the body through an artery called the aorta. In this way, the left ventricle acts like a circulation pump.

As a person gains weight, her body gets bigger, creating more area through which the heart must circulate blood. To get blood through this extra body mass, the left ventricle must pump harder and harder. The ven-

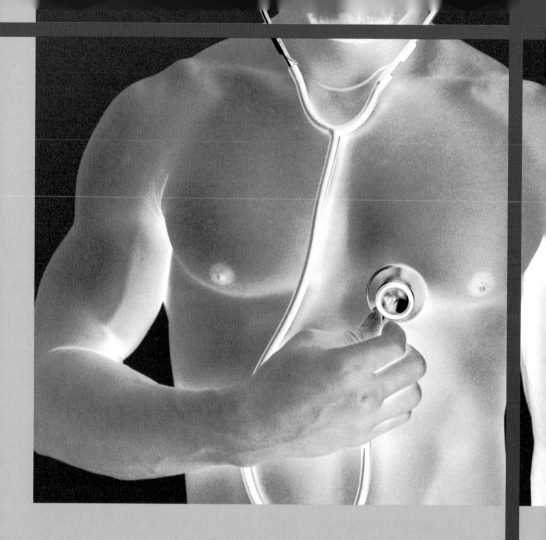

tricle enlarges from working so hard, much like any muscle would enlarge if overly exercised. The ventricle's walls thicken, making it more difficult for the heart to contract properly. This condition is known as left ventricular **hypertrophy**, and it is potentially fatal. Another fatal condition, heart failure, in which the heart can no longer pump enough blood to meet body demands, can also result.

Structural changes in the heart, though well understood, are not the only ways that excess weight contributes to cardiovascular diseases. There are numerous theories regarding the other, less-understood ways in which excess weight affects the cardiovascular system. For example, in January 2004, the *Journal of Clinical Endocrinology and Metabolism* published a university study that showed obese people (those with BMIs over thirty) carry massive amounts of hyperactive oxygen molecules (a type of "*free radical*") in their blood. Based on this information, researchers theorized that excess fat, particularly visceral fat, generates large quantities of these molecules and releases them into the bloodstream. These hyperactive molecules alter the bloodstream and damage arterial walls. Such free radicals, the theory continues, also contribute to fatty deposits in the arteries, which eventually block blood flow.

Another hypothesis regarding excess weight's role in cardiovascular disease concerns the food choices we make. According to the theory, cardiovascular disease is caused largely by specific "bad" foods (such as high-fat foods). Many of these foods also cause weight gain, but the cardiovascular ailments are actually the result of the foods themselves rather than of excess weight. One of the major ways certain foods influence heart healthiness is through

The Good, the Bad, and the Artery

Not all cholesterol is alike. Low-density lipoproteins (LDL; "bad" cholesterol) stick to artery walls, build up, and create clogs. High-density lipoproteins (HDL; "good" cholesterol) actually bind with the LDL molecules, keeping them from sticking to artery walls.

their effect on cholesterol levels. Some foods can raise harmful low-density lipoproteins (also known as LDL or "bad" cholesterol) and lower beneficial high-density lipoproteins (also known as HDL or "good" cholesterol). Countless studies have shown the link between heart disease and elevated LDL levels.

Despite the prevalence of theories, doctors just don't know with absolute certainty all the ways that obesity is linked to cardiovascular disease. Statistics, however, leave no room for doubt. Whether the cause is an overexerted left ventricle, free radicals produced by excess fatty tissue, or the work of specific foods, there is no denying that being overweight is a major risk factor for heart disease. And the more overweight one is, the more at risk he or she becomes.

So what exactly is at stake when it comes to your heart's health? Let's examine the most common heart complications obesity creates: coronary artery disease and high blood pressure.

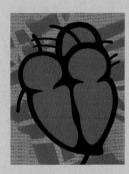

Coronary Artery Disease

According to the Texas Heart Institute, the American Heart Association (AHA), the NIH, and the CDC, coronary artery disease is the leading cause of death in America today. Obesity is a major risk factor for this disease. ("Major" risk factors are those scientists have proven increase the risk of heart disease. "Contributing" risk factors are those that doctors think lead to increased risk.)

What is this killer? Coronary artery disease is a chronic condition in which coronary arteries narrow with blockages and harden. You might have heard of this condition referred to as "hardening of the arteries." Its medical name is atherosclerosis.

How does it work? Think of a drainpipe. When a pipe is free of obstruction, water flows through it with ease. But what if debris builds up along the

inside of the pipe? Maybe rotting leaves, sticks, and trash collect along its sides. Eventually this debris dries and hardens. Then what happens the next time it rains? Rainwater can't pass through the pipe as easily. It may even back up because all kinds of gunk are blocking its way. Outflow becomes but a dribble; little water can get through.

Coronary artery disease works much the same way. Fat and cholesterol molecules carried in the bloodstream stick to artery walls. Eventually these molecules form a waxy, sticky substance called plaque. As blood flows by, this attached plaque snares more and more molecules until a thick buildup occurs. The buildup eventually inhibits or completely blocks blood flow through the artery the same way that debris blocks water flowing through a drain. If oxygen-rich blood can't make it through the arteries to cells and organs, they can fail from oxygen deprivation.

As plaque deposits build up on arterial walls, the arteries begin to harden. This happens because the plaque eventually *calcifies*. Did you ever leave water in a hose in winter? What happens when the water freezes? The hose becomes rigid. Arteries become similarly rigid when their contents solidify. Normally our arteries are muscular and flexible. With each surge of blood pumped by the heart, the arteries expand, allowing large amounts of blood to flow. A hardened artery no longer expands and flexes with each blood surge, thereby limiting how much blood it can accommodate. Each heartbeat is therefore less efficient (because less blood can flow through the arteries with each beat), and the heart must work even harder to get blood where it needs to go. It also has to pump the blood through debris lining the arteries. Talk about a double-whammy!

In addition to the problems plaque causes along our artery walls, sometimes sticky masses break free. These clots then travel throughout the bloodstream and can lodge in arteries elsewhere in the body, blocking blood flow. The result can be a stroke, heart attack, or *embolism*, all of which can be devastating.

Coronary artery disease develops gradually, but make no mistake: it is deadly. The good news, however, is that by losing even five percent of excess fat, by reducing *saturated fats*, *trans-fatty acids*, and cholesterol in one's diet, and by getting regular exercise, a person can lower or even eliminate her risk of developing the disease.

For those already diagnosed with coronary artery disease, a variety of treatment options exist. Noninvasive treatments include what we just mentioned: losing weight and restoring BMI to 25 or lower; limiting saturated fats and cholesterol intake; and getting regular, sustained aerobic exercise.

Invasive treatments include various medications to control cholesterol and break up plaque deposits, *catheter*-based procedures like balloon angioplasty in which a tiny object is inserted into the artery and then expanded to open a clogged passageway, and heart surgery like bypass procedures in which arteries from other parts of the body are inserted to create a "detour" around a blocked passageway. Whatever the means, any blockage must be removed or bypassed or the condition can prove fatal.

High Blood Pressure

Another serious and extremely common form of cardiovascular disease is high blood pressure (also called hypertension). Each time your heart beats, it pushes blood through approximately 60,000 miles (about 96,600 kilometers) of blood vessels. The pressure on blood vessel walls as blood pushes through them coupled with blood vessels' natural resistance to blood flow creates what we know as blood pressure. It is a measure of the force your blood exerts on vessel walls when your heart pumps.

Perhaps it is easiest to understand high blood pressure as simply having an overworked heart and overstressed blood vessels. If the pressure is too great, then it can damage (or even rupture) tiny blood vessels, especially in your eyes, brain, kidneys, and heart. Consequently, monitoring blood pressure is essential for everyone, but particularly for those who are overweight or obese since they're at greater risk for high blood pressure. Once considered an adult problem, doctors now see many cases in children and youth. In fact, an estimated 10 percent of U.S. children have high blood pressure, and obesity causes the overwhelming majority of such cases.

As with coronary artery disease, the precise cause of hypertension is unknown, yet one of three of the following situations usually exists: blood vessels are too narrow, which makes the heart work harder to push blood

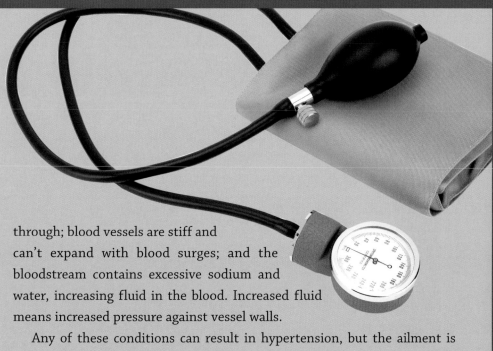

through; blood vessels are stiff and can't expand with blood surges; and the bloodstream contains excessive sodium and water, increasing fluid in the blood. Increased fluid means increased pressure against vessel walls.

Any of these conditions can result in hypertension, but the ailment is most commonly associated with the narrowing of arteries excess weight causes. As arteries gradually narrow with attached plaque, the heart can only get blood through if it pumps with excessive force. Blood pressure rises with each heartbeat and falls with each lull between beats as your heart relaxes. Blood pressure fluctuates minute to minute, changing not only with activity and rest but also with temperature, emotions, posture, and diet. So how can we accurately measure it?

When a medical professional wraps a blood-pressure cuff around your arm and inflates it, the pressure in the cuff temporarily stops blood flow through your arm. When the cuff begins to deflate, gradually releasing this pressure, blood can start to flow again. The person taking your blood pressure listens with a *stethoscope* for the first full pulse of blood flow, noting the pressure at which it began. That measurement is the systolic pressure, the peak pressure created by each heartbeat.

As pressure from the cuff lessens, audibility of the pulse wanes. When all pulse sounds disappear, examiners note that pressure measurement. This is diastolic pressure, the pressure on the blood vessels when the heart relaxes between beats.

> *Today's typical twelve-year-old weighs 11.7 pounds more than his or her counterpart of thirty years ago.*

Blood pressure is measured in a unit called millimeters of mercury (or mm Hg), and the top number is the systolic pressure (peak pressure); the bottom number is the diastolic pressure (resting pressure). A normal or healthy blood pressure for people eighteen and over is 120/80 mm Hg or below. Borderline high blood pressure, also called pre-hypertension, is defined as 121–130 (systolic) over 81–89 (diastolic). High blood pressure (or hypertension) is diagnosed for readings of 140/90 and above. A doctor will usually average at least three blood pressure measurements taken at different times before making a diagnosis of hypertension.

Measuring blood pressure in children and adolescents isn't as straightforward. "Normal" blood pressure in children varies according to height and age. Physicians also take into consideration the fact that children and teens express emotional extremes, which affects blood pressure. If blood pressure is only temporarily high, treatment is not needed. When blood pressure levels are consistently high, hypertension is the likely diagnosis, and treatment begins.

How do physicians treat hypertension? The courses of action are usually the same for adults and kids: lose weight, normalize BMI, cut back on dietary fats and cholesterol, and get plenty of exercise. Doctors usually don't initially prescribe medication unless the patient has significant hypertension (quite high) or organ damage. Weight loss, diet, and exercise are the preferred regimens. They successfully control most cases of hypertension.

Why is lowering high blood pressure so important? Your heart beats an

average of 100,000 times per day. If it's beating with excessive force (as indicated by high blood pressure), it hammers away at your blood vessels with relentless pulses of extreme pressure. That's 100,000 daily opportunities for high blood pressure to wreak its damage. No wonder it kills.

Clearly, heart disease of any kind is dangerous, but in many cases it is also preventable. Thankfully, sometimes heart disease can even be reversed. When a person is diagnosed with a heart disease like coronary artery disease or high blood pressure, she must remember that it's not too late to make improvements in her heart health. Any weight loss, any increase in exercise, and any heart-healthy diet modifications, no matter how small or gradual,

Just five to ten extra pounds can undermine cardiac health.

> *"The trouble with heart disease is that the first symptom is often hard to deal with: sudden death."*
> —Michael Phelps, M.D.

can actually reverse some ravages of heart disease. Cardiovascular benefits are apparent once you expend just 500 Calories per week in exercise. That's equivalent to just two hours of moderately paced walking or under an hour of moderately paced aerobics. So get off that couch and get moving!

One last thought: If 70 percent of all cardiovascular disease is related to excess weight, and cardiovascular disease kills, then indirectly, obesity kills, too. Don't minimize its risks. The cost is too great.

When we discuss Calories in food, we talk about Calories with a capital "C". This stands for kilocalorie. It's the amount of energy needed to heat one kilogram of water (approximately 1 liter or 4.25 cups) one degree Celsius. A small calorie, or calorie with a lower-case "c," is the amount of energy needed to heat one gram of water (approximately 1 millimeter or 20 drops from an eyedropper) one degree Celsius. There are one thousand small calories in one food Calorie.

Chapter 4

A Stealthy Invader: Cancer

- Breast Cancer
- Colon (Colorectal) Cancer
- Esophageal Cancer
- Other Cancers

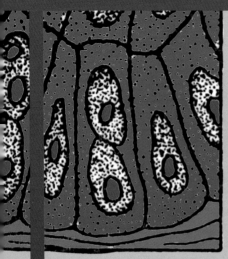
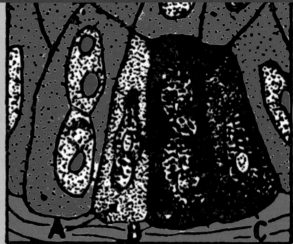

Think for a moment about the following statistics. Women who gain forty-four pounds or more after the age of eighteen double their risk of breast cancer, and half of all breast cancer cases in *postmenopausal* women occur in those who are obese. Large waist size (abdominal obesity) is associated with *colorectal* cancer. The higher a person's BMI is, the greater his likelihood of developing *esophageal* cancer. The American Cancer Society attributes undesirable dietary practices and resulting weight issues to nearly one-third of the 500,000 annual cancer deaths in the United States alone. That's 167,000 deaths.

Granted, the relationship between obesity and cancer is mostly statistical. The numbers show that obese people suffer from greater cancer rates, but a direct cause and effect relationship has yet to be proven or understood. Nevertheless, study after study confirms a link exists. The first studies associating obesity with cancer began as early as the 1940s. Over the decades since then, medical opinions have shifted back and forth regarding any relationship, but current wisdom supports a definite connection.

For example, the American Cancer Society recently concluded a large, long-term study of this connection and found increased rates of kidney, stomach, and uterine cancers among the obese. It also found increased rates of cancers like colon, rectal, and prostate in men; and cervical, ovarian, gallbladder, and breast in women. Clearly researchers see an association, but they don't understand exactly why it exists.

That's not surprising when you realize that not all cancers are alike. Each form is a unique disease in and of itself. Individual types of cancer exhibit distinct cellular characteristics, progress at certain speeds, respond to different therapies, and metastasize (spread) to different sites. Why? As of yet, no one really knows. The profiles of each cancer and each person with cancer are simply too varied to draw any single conclusion. For example, environmental exposure might explain one malignancy, while genetic factors or lifestyle determine another. Or a combination of known and unknown elements may be the culprit. Given all conceivable causes of cancer, isolating one specific cause with absolute certainty becomes practically impossible. And if we don't know exactly what causes cancer, then understanding why the obese develop cancer more often also becomes impossible.

Despite not understanding the why and how of obesity's relationship to cancer, we do know that a relationship exists. People suffering from obesity are at an increased risk of developing specific types of cancer. What kinds of cancer does obesity effect? Let's look at the most common.

Breast Cancer

Many studies have found that obesity impacts breast cancer two ways. First, it tremendously increases the postmenopausal woman's risk of getting the disease, and second, it increases the likelihood she won't survive. (Obesity lowers survival rates, not only of cancer, but also of many health conditions.)

The main reason for increased fatality rates is that excess fat obscures and delays discovery of the tumors. A recent Yale University study found that severely obese men and women are three times more likely to have breast tumors detected later (yes, men can get breast cancer, too) and at less-treatable stages of the disease. Tragically, by the time tumors are large

Surprise!

Obesity increases the risk of breast cancer in men as well as women.

Weight gain during adulthood is the most consistent and strongest predictor of breast cancer risk.

(Source: The National Cancer Institute)

enough to detect through layers of fatty tissue, it's often too late. The cancer has spread.

Another factor in these high death rates is that obese men and women tend not to survive major surgery as well as people with a healthy weight. And cancer often requires surgery. However, fat per se is not the direct cause of such frailty. A host of obesity-related complications like high blood pressure, heart disease, and diabetes are usually to blame.

One National Cancer Institute (NCI) report cited that 14 percent of annual cancer deaths in men and 20 percent in women were due to being overweight and obese. More specifically, scientists estimate that up to 18,000 deaths per year from breast cancer (in patients over fifty) could be avoided if these men and women could maintain a BMI under twenty-five throughout their adult lives.

For women, the overall effect of obesity on potential breast cancer depends largely on menopausal status. Interestingly, before menopause obese women have a lower risk of developing breast cancer than women of healthy weight. However, after menopause, obese women jump to twice the risk.

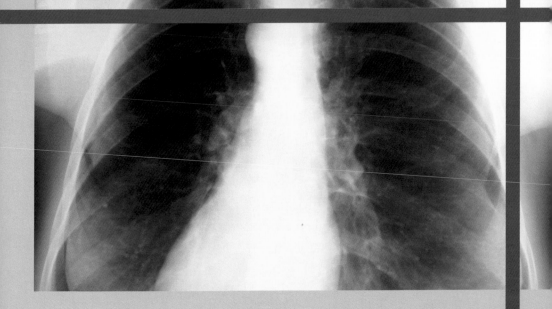

Estrogen seems to be the culprit. Before menopause, the ovaries are the primary source of estrogen, but fatty tissue also produces it. After menopause, when ovaries stop producing this hormone, fatty tissue becomes the main estrogen source. Consequently, estrogen levels in post-menopausal, heavy women can be twice as high as that of their lean counter-parts. High estrogen levels after menopause seem to play an important role in the development of breast cancer, but again, researchers don't know why.

Colon (Colorectal) Cancer

Although men can develop breast cancer, the rates are obviously many times higher in women. But colon cancer (which can also develop in women) occurs at much higher rates in men. The colon is commonly referred to as the large intestine, and men with a BMI over 25 have an increased risk of developing cancer in this organ. Study after study consistently reports such findings, but like so much of what we've discussed so far, the medical community still can't say precisely why.

Researchers have proposed a number of ideas concerning obesity's effect on colon-cancer risk. One major theory suggests that high levels of insulin in obese people may promote the growth of tumors. Another theory concerns diet. A diet low in fiber has also been linked to an increased risk of colon cancer. Fiber is most plentiful in certain vegetables, fruits, legumes, and whole grains. All of these foods also tend to be extremely healthy and low in fat. Many people develop overweight and obesity at least in part because of unhealthy diets. If the unhealthy diet that contributed to the weight gain was also low in fiber (as most unhealthy diets are), could this be the reason for the increased risk for colon cancer? Some researchers believe so. But if things like insulin or diets are responsible for the relationship between colon cancer and obesity, why wouldn't colon cancer appear at equal rates among obese men and women? Researchers have a theory about this too.

Some researchers theorize that, as with breast cancer, estrogen may be playing a role in colon-cancer rates in obese women. However, in the case of colon cancer, estrogen may actually be having an opposite effect. It may actually protect against colon-cancer development whereas it spurs breast-cancer development. As we already learned, excess fat later in life translates into more estrogen. So, while this increased estrogen greatly increases a woman's risk of developing breast cancer, it seems to reduce her risk of developing colon cancer. In the end, estrogen may be responsible for the differences in colon cancer rates in men and women.

Esophageal Cancer

According to the NCI, overweight and obese people are twice as likely as healthy-weight people to develop esophageal cancer (cancer of the esophagus). As with the other cancers we have discussed thus far, however, the reason excess weight influences these *carci-*

nomas is not yet understood. One theory proposes that the increased cancer risk may be linked to gastric reflux.

Gastric reflux, also called acid reflux, occurs when digestive fluids back up out of the stomach and into the esophagus. This acid overflow can cause symptoms like a burning sensation in the upper abdomen, chest, and/or back (also known as heartburn), burning in the throat, sour taste in the mouth, and belching. When stomach acid backs up, it damages the delicate tissues that line the esophagus (hence the burning sensation). Many researchers believe that this damage, if repeated over time, may eventually cause cancer. Being overweight or obese increases one's likelihood of developing acid reflux because the extra weight puts pressure on the stomach, constricting its size and pushing fluid up into the esophagus. Many researchers thus conclude that this increased tendency for acid reflux also explains the increased esophageal cancer rates in overweight and obese men and women.

Other Cancers

Breast, colorectal, and esophageal are probably the three most common cancers impacted by obesity. But other types of cancer seem to be influenced as well. Here is a partial list of these cancers and their respective statistics. All facts come from the NIH, the CDC, or the NCI.

Endometrial (Uterine) Cancer

- Women suffering from obesity have up to four times the probability of developing this type of cancer than women with normal BMIs.
- Body size is a risk factor regardless of where the fat is concentrated.
- Obesity accounts for about 40 percent of endometrial cancer cases.

Kidney (Renal Cell) Cancer

- Consistent evidence shows a clear link between this cancer and obesity, some studies say especially in women.
- People who are overweight have about a 36 percent higher risk for developing renal cell cancer. People who are obese are at an increased risk of 84 percent.
- Excess weight (either overweight or obese) accounts for up to 21 percent of all renal cell cancer cases.

Pancreatic Cancer

- Evidence is mixed.
- One recent analysis reported that obese people have a 19 percent higher risk of pancreatic cancer than those with a healthy BMI.
- Another study found that obesity only increases this type of cancer risk in those who are also not physically active.

Gallbladder Cancer

- The risk of this cancer is largely associated with gallstones.
- Because the obese tend to encounter a higher frequency of gallstones, their risk of gallbladder cancer increases as well.

Let's be clear: the medical community does not yet understand exactly how obesity increases any of these cancers' incidence. It just sees case after case supporting a connection. Frankly, the mechanism by which excess fat triggers these diseases likely differs from cancer to cancer, so it's hard to track down. But let's leave the why and how to the experts' examination. For the average person, they are unimportant. Knowing obesity elevates cancer risk is enough for us. How can we avoid such risk?

Most responsible guidelines for cancer prevention include two basic principles: eat a wide variety of foods in moderation and prevent obesity through diet and exercise. Remember, a healthy BMI is between 18.5 and 24.9. What steps should you take to achieve these numbers? Experts recommend establishing healthy eating and physical activity early in life. Lifelong habits are often formed during adolescence, so it's never too early to start entrenching healthy lifestyle choices. For those who are already overweight or obese, the first thing to do is avoid gaining any additional weight. The next goal should be to shed some of the extra pounds. Although it's not clear how much weight loss is needed to begin decreasing cancer risk, we have already learned that losing just five percent of body weight can provide significant health benefits. Losing weight is certainly difficult for many people. Numerous diets, programs, and products abound promising weight-loss miracles, but don't be

fooled. Most doctors agree that for the majority of people the most successful and healthiest road to weight loss is still a healthy diet and increased exercise. Discussing one's weight-loss goals and options with a health professional is often the best first step to getting on the road to better health.

Cancer is a scary thing. Most people tense at the mere mention of the "c" word. While experts cannot definitively say why being overweight or obese raises the risk of cancer, the statistics are undeniable: cancer and excess weight are linked! What is the cost here? From a strictly physical standpoint, grave illness or even death. Now think of the possible emotional and social effects of cancer, like becoming depressed, being too sick to work, and being isolated from family and friends. Losing a few pounds suddenly doesn't seem so bad!

Chapter 5

Aching and Exhausted: Osteoarthritis and Sleep Apnea

- Osteoarthritis

- Sleep Apnea

Cindy is only twenty-five, but she feels eighty. Her joints ache, especially her hips and knees. On bad days, just walking can be difficult, let alone going up and down stairs. *Your twenties aren't supposed to feel this way*, she despairs. *I'm still young, so why does my body feel so old?*

On top of her aches and pains, Cindy experiences frequent daytime sleepiness. In fact, she feels tired all the time. *Maybe I'm not sleeping well and just don't remember it,* she considers. *Or maybe something's really wrong.*

Cindy is extremely concerned about her symptoms and what they might mean for her health, but she's blind to her overall fitness. Her BMI is thirty-two—technically obese—and she's sporting an extra thirty pounds. Plus her once-active lifestyle has become largely sedentary. No wonder her joints hurt! If you were in Cindy's situation, your joints would probably hurt too. Carrying that much extra weight makes Cindy's knees pinch and throb when she walks or runs, so any unnecessary activity is out. (Her motto is: Avoid pain at all costs!) But by limiting her activity, Cindy is compounding her weight troubles. With every added pound, her knees hurt even more, and with each additional stab of pain, she moves less. With every decrease in activity, her weight increases, and the cycle continues.

Cindy's situation is not uncommon. By deceiving herself (or being in genuine *ignorance* about her situation) she fails to acknowledge that the extra load she's carrying could explain her aches and exhaustion. Her first symptom, aching joints, is due to a condition called osteoarthritis. Her exhaustion is due to a condition called sleep apnea.

Osteoarthritis

Osteoarthritis, also called "degenerative joint disease," is the most common joint disorder. It occurs when cartilage, the slippery, cushioning material that covers the ends of bones in a joint, breaks down (or degenerates). Healthy cartilage allows bones to glide back and forth over one another. It also absorbs shock from the impact of physical movement. In osteoarthritis, layers of cartilage wear away making the cushioning thinner and less effective. If osteoarthritis becomes serious enough, bone will meet bone, causing decreased movement and pain. Osteoarthritis is usually the worst in joints that bear the most weight, specifically the knees, hips, and lower back.

Osteoarthritis is primarily linked with aging, and all of us experience it to some degree (whether or not it becomes serious enough to cause pain). Older people naturally develop the condition after decades of bodily wear and tear, but overweight and obese individuals typically experience its debilitating effects at much younger ages. That makes sense when you think about it. Your musculoskeletal system (your bones, muscles, and connective tissues like ligaments and tendons) is designed to carry a healthy amount of weight over the course of your lifetime. With normal usage, this system should serve you well and be relatively trouble free for at least six decades. If you tax joints with a greater load than they are meant to bear, however, those joints wear out sooner than they otherwise would. You could compare this to the brake pads on a car.

When you step on your car's brake, the brake pads press against the spinning tires, causing friction that slows the wheels. If enough pressure is applied, the car's movement eventually stops. This friction is hard on the brake pads, and they wear away a little with each use. Nevertheless, brake pads are built to withstand a certain amount of pressure and friction, and if used properly, they will have a relatively long life. If forced to endure extra pressure and friction constantly, however (such as when you slam on your breaks or "ride" the brake when going downhill) the pads will wear out faster than they are meant to. Of course, when it comes to a car, you're lucky. When your brake pads wear out, you can just get new ones. Your joints don't work this way. You can't grow new cartilage. When it's gone, it's gone for good.

WHEEL BRAKE

What are the signs that osteoarthritis is setting in? Obviously pain is the most common symptom, particularly in weight-bearing joints and after repetitive use. Make no mistake about it: When bone starts to rub against bone, whether in your vertebrae or knee, it hurts! Swelling, inflammation, and loss of flexibility also mark this disease.

Unfortunately, losing weight cannot reverse any damage osteoarthritis inflicts, but it can alleviate some pain, improve flexibility, and decrease the degeneration rate. Consequently, weight loss is usually the first course of treatment. It can make a substantial impact on comfort, function, and the course of the disease.

Physicians will also usually recommend range-of-motion exercises and muscle-strengthening work under the watchful eye of a physical therapist. For pain, something as simple as two Tylenol® (acetaminophen) or a heating pad can make a world of difference, but doctors might also prescribe a mild *narcotic* painkiller or *nonsteroidal anti-inflammatory medications* like high-dose ibuprofen (Motrin®) to take off the edge.

These courses of treatment effectively manage arthritis for most people. For some, only more extreme measures work. Injecting anti-inflammatory hormones (also called corticosteroids) directly into the joint is one common

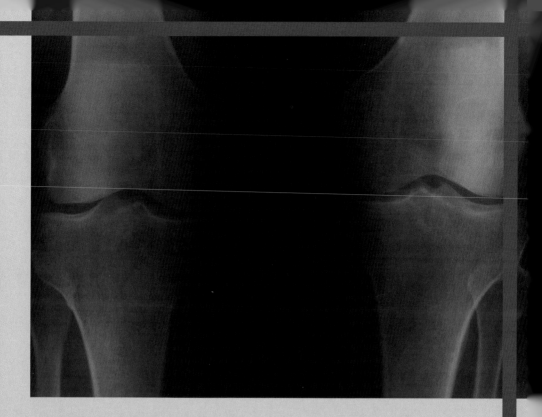

short-term treatment, but doctors usually limit these shots to only two or three treatments per year.

Surgery is another option. Surgery to resurface (smooth out) bones, reposition bones, or simply remove loose pieces of cartilage from the joint if they are causing mechanical symptoms like pinching, buckling, or locking are not uncommon. The most extreme procedure is joint-replacement surgery, but your doctor would likely recommend less-drastic measures first. All surgery has risks, and as you learned in chapter 4, people suffering from obesity have a more difficult time recovering after surgery and are also more likely to die from surgery-related complications. Weight loss (to a healthy BMI) at the onset of symptoms, or even before, is perhaps the safest and most effective treatment for early osteoarthritis.

So, if Cindy shed that extra thirty pounds, her knees would feel much better. Then she'd be able to restore her active lifestyle, which would, in turn, help her maintain a healthy BMI. Exercise and a healthy diet might also increase her energy level. But lack of physical activity isn't the only thing that's making Cindy tired. If you remember from the beginning of the chapter, there's another condition we said Cindy is suffering from. It's called sleep apnea.

Sleep Apnea

"It started harmlessly enough. I felt a little more tired than usual. Sometimes I couldn't concentrate in class, and my memory seemed off a bit. Then I started nodding off during lectures. If the room was warm and the prof droned on, down I went. *It's not my fault*, I'd rationalize. *The building needs air conditioning, and a university this size should be able to afford more dynamic teachers.* I could come up with an explanation for any symptom. I never saw the pattern."—Ron, a college freshman

"I've actually known I have sleep apnea for years; I just haven't done anything about it. When I was living at home, my dad used to tell me that I stopped breathing during the night and that he would actually count the seconds until I started to breathe again. At the time I thought I was sleeping soundly—I never remembered waking up—so I never gave it a second thought.

"Then came college. Every one of my roommates hounded me about snoring. Apparently I can bring down the roof with one good nap. *So what?* I'd silently respond. *I snore, and occasionally I stop breathing for a few seconds. At least I'm getting some sleep.* (That's more than I could say about a lot of them!)

"But now I'm noticing that I'm really tired a lot, particularly during the afternoon and at the end of the day. I need to take lots of naps, and I've even caught myself falling asleep at the wheel. That's crazy. Maybe this sleep stuff is more serious than I thought." —Kyle, a twenty-something professional

The Greek word "apnea" means "without breath." People with sleep apnea literally stop breathing—are without breath—repeatedly during their sleep. In some cases, this happens literally hundreds of times per night and often for thirty seconds or longer! These periods of not breathing often wake the person from deep sleep, the kind of sleep that restores us. How can anyone get any rest with all those interruptions?

In the world of sleep disorders, there are basically two main types of sleep apnea: obstructive apnea and central apnea. Fully nine out of ten people with sleep apnea have obstructive apnea. It is also the type of sleep apnea affected by obesity, so we'll limit our discussion to obstructive apnea.

If you have obstructive apnea, something is blocking your trachea (the passageway, commonly referred to as the windpipe, that brings air in and out of your body) while you sleep. Normally when a person sleeps, his throat muscles stay sufficiently tense to keep the airway open. A person suffering from sleep apnea, however, experiences a relaxation of the throat muscles while he sleeps. This relaxation allows a blockage to form in the passageway.

Many things, such as your tongue, tonsils, uvula (that dangly thing in the back of your throat), soft tissue in the back of the throat, the relaxed throat muscles themselves, or fatty tissue can cause such a blockage. Whatever the culprit, the sleeper keeps trying to breathe, but he can't get enough air because something is in the way. After usually twenty to thirty seconds, the sleeper is disturbed enough to rouse, throat muscles contract, and the throat reopens. Normal air exchange resumes, the individual falls back to sleep, throat muscles relax again allowing the blockage to move back into place, and the cycle repeats.

Why are the overweight and obese at increased risk of developing this sleep disorder? Extra fatty tissue, particularly if distributed on the upper body, may be responsible for collapsing the airway. A person who is overweight can have fat stored around his neck. This concentration of fatty tissue can compress and narrow the airway, making it more difficult to breathe to begin with. Then those throat muscles relax. The added weight of the excess fat makes the airway more likely to collapse.

Is sleep apnea dangerous? To many people, the condition seems harmless, but don't be so quick to write off this disorder. The more serious one's sleep apnea is, the greater the risks can be, especially if disturbed sleep at night leads to exhaustion during the day. If you suffer from sleep apnea, perhaps your greatest risk is getting behind the wheel of a car. Falling asleep at the wheel kills thousands every year. You're more likely to have a serious acci-

"A healthy body is the guest chamber of the soul; a sick body, its prison."
—Francis Bacon, U.S. Business Executive (*Augmentis Scientiarum*)

dent if you drive when sleepy, and you're more likely to be sleepy on a regular basis if you have sleep apnea. Job or school performance can also suffer as mental *acuity* decreases with lack of rest.

Sleep apnea, however, can have more direct health risks. If left untreated, sleep apnea can lead to high blood pressure, other forms of cardiovascular disease, memory issues, impotency, headaches, and weight gain. In extremely serious (but also extremely rare) cases, death can even result. Fortunately, doctors can easily diagnose and treat sleep apnea. In fact, simply losing weight corrects this disorder in 90 percent of patients.

So what costs of being overweight have we found in this chapter? Osteoarthritis is both painful and debilitating. A person suffering from osteoarthritis simply can't live as she used to. Even routine tasks like shopping, walking to get the mail, or getting in and out of a car become a challenge. Every move causes discomfort.

Sleep apnea impacts us in ways we probably don't even realize. It's easy to downplay being tired, but when you're tired, you can't think straight or function properly. Job or school performance can suffer as one's memory and clarity of thought muddles. Relationships can also suffer because one may simply be more irritable and moody. Eventually depression can set in.

Chapter 6

Weighing on Your Mind: The Psychological Impact

- Psychosocial Issues

- Neurochemical and Genetic Components

Ali Schmidt is five-feet, seven-inches tall, athletic, and slim. She's attractive, popular, and accomplished, and she usually loves going back to school each fall. But last September was different. Ali was not only starting a new school, she was attending as a "fat girl."

As part of an experiment designed to reveal the emotional and psychological impact of obesity, Ali agreed to spend two days pretending to be someone she's not. The experiment turned Ali into a 200-pound "new girl" entering Connecticut's Stratford High School. (Ali is from the Bronx, New York.) The results of the experiment were recorded for the ABC News special *Fat Like Me*.

At the start of the experiment, Ali was packed in padding called a "fat suit." Using latex and makeup similar to that used on Gwyneth Paltrow in the film *Shallow Hal*, special-effects artists completed Ali's transformation. Her new look was both dramatic and convincing. Ali was literally a thin person trapped in a fat person's body. And she hated it.

"I felt pain that was excruciating," she lamented after the first day. "Walking down the halls was like walking into hell." Kids with whom Ali otherwise might have made friends—if she hadn't been in the fat suit—put her down or dismissed her with just one glance. Some were downright rude.

"I wanted them to realize that I wasn't who I appeared to be."

Students laughed behind her back, and others made mean remarks. In either case, Ali was the object of their ridicule after only one day. That hurt. Ali felt singled out and isolated. She had never experienced anything remotely like it in her "thin" life.

"They're just complete jerks to you," she admitted. "People don't go, 'Ha, ha, you're white,' or 'Ha, ha, you're black,' but they see a fat person and they think that they have the right to laugh at them."

In just two days, Ali Schmidt developed a new awareness of and sensitivity to the plight of overweight people everywhere. Fortunately for her, she could take off her fat suit at the end of the day. But for her obese peers, ABC News' experiment is an unrelenting, daily reality that cannot so easily be escaped.

Psychosocial Issues

So far in this book we've discussed many physical costs of being overweight, but what about the psychological impact? The emotional scars some kids carry into adulthood are just as debilitating as any physical disease.

Americans, although the heaviest people on earth, are also some of the most image conscious. Our television programs, movies, magazines, and advertisements are plastered with pictures of incredibly thin, tall, toned, tan, flawless bodies. We've set beauty standards so high that practically no one can achieve them. Clearly, being overweight in image-crazed America is a tremendous source of frustration, dissatisfaction, and yes, even depression. The fact is that our society does view excess weight negatively and judgmentally. Discrimination—from school to the workplace, from clothing to the travel industry—is everywhere. It's wrong, but all too real.

For years professionals and *laypeople* alike assumed that people who were overweight or obese were lazy, stupid, undisciplined, and *gluttonous*. Although many people now realize this is not the case, American society in general still has a very negative attitude toward people carrying excess weight. More often than not, those who struggle with weight internalize society's views. This results in self-disdain, especially in

people in their teens, twenties, or thirties. Overweight individuals commonly think they're defective or somehow less valuable than their "normal-weight" peers. Such feelings, particularly if ongoing, can even escalate into clinical depression.

Interestingly, researchers have found that most people who are overweight aren't "down" or "anxious" about their weight per se, but about dieting, the pressure to diet, diet failures, and what others think. That's a subtle, but noteworthy distinction. It means that many people wouldn't automatically feel badly about their weight and themselves if it weren't for the negative reactions of others. These anxieties can affect people's lives in many ways. For example, many people experiencing excess weight are extremely self-conscious about eating in public. Many "normal-weight" people don't think twice about it.

Whether self-motivated or stemming from others' reactions, people struggling with excess weight often develop a negative body image. Body image develops in response to how you perceive your physical self and the effects these perceptions have on the way you feel about yourself. For example, if you see your body as healthy, strong, and capable of doing many things, you will likely feel very good about your body and have a positive body image. (A healthy body image is also an important element in building positive self-esteem.) If you see your body as weak, clumsy, and unattractive, you will probably feel badly about yourself and develop a negative body image. It is important to remember that body image is not necessarily based on the way your body *truly* is. It is based on the way you *believe* your body is. A person, therefore, may have an extremely healthy, strong body yet still suffer from a negative body image.

Typically, overweight and obese people tend to be less accurate than people of a "normal" weight when evaluating their own size and appearance. People carrying excess weight generally overestimate their body size by 6 to 12 percent. In short, they think they're bigger than they actually are. This warped self-perception may be the result of social influences that proclaim heavier bodies to be worse, less attractive, or less valuable than thinner bodies.

When overweight persons react so strongly and negatively to their appearance, the reaction often overshadows all of their other characteristics or accomplishments, no matter how noteworthy. Many people are blinded by their weight, becoming overwhelmingly preoccupied with their appearance and blocking out the more-positive feelings important to healthy self-esteem.

Consider Amy, an award-winning professional artist from New York. Recently, she received two gold awards for excellence in design at the New York Annual Art Directors Awards Show. The honor is akin to winning the Oscar® for best actress. Yet Amy was miserable when she found out she'd have to accept the award in front of hundreds of other designers. "How can I stand in front of all those people when I'm this heavy? They probably don't think I deserve the award anyway."

Depending on the frequency and intensity of these feelings, an over-weight person may isolate himself from social situations, especially ones linked to eating or appearance (like attending an awards dinner or shopping for clothes with friends). In these arenas, any outgoing personality traits often lose out to self-consciousness. Sometimes the barrier, though, is

Fighting Back

Not all obese people are depressed about or unhappy with their weight. Take, for example, the Clydesdales, an international group (six countries including Canada and the United States currently have clubs) committed to athletic opportunities for large competitors. Its motto is: "You don't need to be thin to be healthy," and its members (all of whom are technically overweight and obese) compete in marathons, duathlons, and triathlons.

"I walked into a popular restaurant the evening after I ran the Boston Marathon," shared one Clydesdale. "Some teen guys were there who made a few rude remarks about my size. They spoke under their breath, but I heard every word.

"So I walked up to them and asked them if they had any idea what I did that day? After a few nervous chuckles and a couple of bad jokes, they admitted they didn't. I told them that I had completed the Boston Marathon in under four hours. Then I asked them if they could do that. That shut them up."

strictly physical. Negotiating stairs, cars, and a world designed for the thin just takes too much effort, so people whose weight makes these situations challenging or uncomfortable may stay home.

The negative psychological impacts that weight issues can bring don't affect everyone equally. Men and the elderly seem to be more accepting of themselves and less concerned with weight matters, eating, and appearance. Women and young people, however, report varying degrees of distress, ranging from feeling self-conscious or unattractive to feeling downright rejected or suicidal. In fact, according to the *Archives of Pediatric and Adolescent Medicine*, a University of Minnesota study of 5,000 teenagers found that 26 percent of those who were teased at school and at home about their weight had considered suicide, and 9 percent (that's almost one in ten) had actually attempted to kill themselves. Thirty-six percent of teased girls and 19 percent of teased boys reported being depressed.

Neurochemical and Genetic Components

Americans are slowly, very slowly, catching on that many social stigmas attached to obesity only reveal misinformation and ignorance. People with overweight or obesity are not necessarily lazy or undisciplined, and they certainly aren't stupid. Yes, lifestyle choices (food selection and activity level) can cause excess weight in some people, but they aren't the cause for everyone. Some people are just wired to be a larger size. More and more evidence suggests that biochemical and genetic components play a greater role in being overweight than traditionally believed.

Obesity is a complex condition, and it varies from individual to individual. Some people can attain a healthier weight by cutting down on certain foods and getting more exercise. For this population, diet and exercise are proper interventions because they work. But there are also many overweight

people whose bodies do not respond to such seemingly logical approaches. (We all know someone who has diligently tried to lose weight, experienced limited success, and then just gained it back again.) Why can some people succeed with diet and exercise while other people fail? The answer may be in the genetic code.

Evidence from twin, adoption, and family studies strongly suggests familial similarities in maintaining body weight. Putting on the pounds is often *hereditary*. Does this mean that those with a susceptible biological predisposition are destined to a life of obesity and its health effects? Not necessarily. No, we can't change our genes, and many people will never be able to achieve their desired thinness no matter how much they try. But as you've learned throughout this book, losing even 5 to 10 percent of total body mass can result in health benefits even if ideal weight remains elusive. Even if we can't give ourselves "thin genes," we can alter our behavior and make health-improving changes to our weight.

The discovery that overweight and obesity can be genetic has both positive and negative psychological *repercussions*. For those who genuinely carry the so-called "fat gene," it's a relief to realize they're not solely responsible for their condition. That's a positive. For those whose weight issues are not genetic, however, blaming biology can confuse the issue and allow people to deny the reality of their health situations. That's a negative. Regardless, recognizing that obesity may be due to a genetically determined *metabolic* condition (rather than character flaws) is important for those affected and for society as a whole.

Recent *neurochemical* research has also shown a physiological link between obesity and depression. It seems that we aren't just depressed because of society's reactions to and our own feelings about our bodies after all. Rather, the same chemical imbalances that usually trigger long-term depression in people of "normal" weight also trigger the food cravings many obese people encounter. The chemical imbalance appears to be depleted serotonin levels in the brain.

Serotonin, a well-established factor in depressive disorders and sleepiness, is a neurotransmitter. Neurotransmitters are chemicals brain cells release to trigger the action of the next brain cell. Once the neurotransmitter has done its work stimulating the next cell, the first cell reabsorbs it to use again. Depleted levels of serotonin occur when cells reabsorb too much serotonin, thereby lessening overall levels in the brain. Consequently, doctors have developed a whole class of medications called selective serotonin reuptake inhibitors (SSRIs) to counteract this effect. They're quite effective.

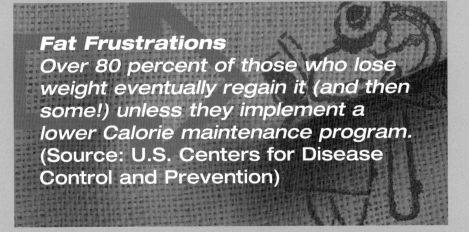

Fat Frustrations
Over 80 percent of those who lose weight eventually regain it (and then some!) unless they implement a lower Calorie maintenance program. (Source: U.S. Centers for Disease Control and Prevention)

What does serotonin have to do with obesity? Depressed people lack serotonin, and recent studies suggest that most obese people lack serotonin as
well. Carbohydrates, however, seem to stimulate serotonin production.
When asked why they eat so much food knowing it'll just compound their
obesity, many people respond that their eating habits have little to do with
hunger or taste. Food actually calms them and reduces their anxiety.
Research proves the claim. In a recent study, when both carb-craving and
non-carb-craving subjects were fed a carbohydrate-rich meal, the cravers'
mood improved for up to three hours after eating. The non-cravers just got
sleepy and felt fatigued. Why?

Studies have shown that an amino acid, tryptophan, increases in the
blood when a person eats carbohydrates. Carbohydrates also stimulate the
secretion of insulin, which speeds the uptake of tryptophan into the central
nervous system. The tryptophan is then converted to serotonin in the brain.
Based on the fact that many depressed and obese people have low serotonin
levels and carbohydrates can stimulate serotonin production, many
researchers now believe that obese and depressed people are in a sense using
food as a medication. The body recognizes serotonin deficiency and triggers

> *"Beauty comes in all ages, colors, shapes, and forms. God never makes junk."*
> —Kathy Ireland, U.S. Model

the desire for serotonin-friendly foods, specifically carbohydrates. A cycle of feeling blue, craving carbs, eating carbs, feeling better, then feeling blue again sets in. The cycle repeats, and leads to weight gain.

Most overweight people crave (and overeat) carbs more than people of "normal" weight. In fact, researchers estimate that as many as two-thirds of those with BMIs over twenty-five are carbohydrate-cravers. Abnormally low serotonin levels could, in effect, be causing their overweight and obesity. Uncontrollable weight gain might just come down to brain chemistry.

Self-consciousness, isolation, rejection, low self-esteem, distorted body image, self-deprecation, feelings of failure, depression, and even suicide: all can be potential psychological side effects of obesity. Again, not everyone who's overweight or obese ends up feeling this way, but many do, particularly teens and women. The emotional costs for them are huge, and they carry them for a lifetime.

What treatments are available? Obviously, if suicide is even remotely on your mind, see your doctor immediately. You should also see your doctor if you are experiencing depression or persistent negative feelings about yourself. Your doctor will likely refer you to a psychiatrist who may prescribe an SSRI to elevate serotonin levels. Counseling and nutritional assistance are also common and beneficial therapies. And, as shown in every chapter so far, shedding a healthy amount of weight, then maintaining that weight through regular exercise and smart eating habits is perhaps the most effective therapy.

Chapter 7

Weighing the Costs

- A Big Bill

- Protecting Our Most Precious "Commodity"

Warren has type 2 diabetes, a condition that set in after he gained forty pounds in adulthood. His symptoms are severe enough that he monitors his blood-glucose levels several times per day. The machine that does the test costs about $100, which Warren's medical insurance covers. But that's just a fraction of the amount being overweight has cost him.

"I've spent literally thousands of dollars on diet plans, weight-loss foods, health club fees, and even hypnosis. Nothing's worked for long. I always end up gaining back every pound I lose plus a few more. Now I'm heavier than I've ever been, and it may ultimately cost me my life."

A Big Bill

In this book we've covered common physical and psychosocial consequences of obesity. Many people believe excess weight only hurts those who suffer from it. This of course is untrue. The health impact, whether it is physical or psychological, touches not only those actually struggling with these conditions but their families and friends as well. But the effects of overweight and obesity reach further. These effects actually translate into huge monetary costs, and all of society pays that bill. Our wallets, and those of our employers, the medical industry, and the government, all chip in to support the financial burden created by our growing waistlines. The cost of obesity is not just physical; it's hugely financial.

Overweight individuals face a dizzying array of health issues that will cost their families thousands upon thousands of dollars: heart disease, stroke, diabetes, cancer, and arthritis, to name a few. All are directly related to being overweight. The medical costs are staggering. Many families face bankruptcy trying to dig out of the debt-hole one good illness digs. And if a family doesn't have the means to pay, then Medicaid or Medicare kicks in. Such government aid is funded by the taxes we each pay. The more the government

must pay out, the higher our taxes go. Consequently, we all pay for the obesity crisis indirectly.

A new study by researchers at the CDC estimates that U.S. obesity-attributable medical costs reached $75 billion in 2003, and taxpayers footed almost half these costs through Medicare and Medicaid. But direct medical expenses are by no means the only monetary repercussions of overweight and obesity. For example, think about the costs to companies when employees must take off time because of weight-related ailments. The company not only loses the money it pays to the employee while she is on sick leave. There is also the cost of lost productivity—the benefit the company would have received from having that employee at work performing her job. Companies

Company Costs

Annual American workdays lost related to obesity:
  39.3 million
Annual restricted-activity days related to obesity:
  239.0 million
Annual bed-rest days related to obesity:
  89.5 million
Annual physician office visits related to obesity:
  62.7 million
TOTAL COST (in 2001 dollars):
  $3.9 billion
(Source: National Institutes of Health)

The total cost of obesity to U.S. companies is about
  $14 billion per year.
Health Insurance Premiums: $8 billion
Paid Sick Leave: $2.5 billion
Disability Insurance: $1.5 billion
Life Insurance: $2 billion

(Source: The National Business Group on Health)

are paying, but no one is working. In 2002, the cost of lost productivity was estimated at $44.6 billion dollars. Who makes up for the loss? In many cases we, the consumers, pay in increased prices companies must charge to stay profitable.

Even the cost to businesses and productivity, however, do not complete our weight-related bill. Think about the billions of dollars the diet industry rakes in by marketing false hope. Even when we try to remedy our weight problems, it costs us big time. According to the CDC, Americans are currently spending $40 billion per year on dieting and diet-related products. Almost half of American women and one in four men say they're on a diet. Half of American nine- and ten-year-old girls say dieting makes them feel better about themselves. In other words, dieting is no longer the exception; it's become the norm.

Add to that $40 billion the other $75 billion in medical-related costs, and Americans are spending approximately $117 billion a year on their weight issues. According to a recent congressional report, overweight and obese individuals spend more on health services and medications than daily smokers and heavy drinkers combined, a full 77 percent more on medications alone. Only aging has a greater effect.

"Obesity has become a crucial health problem for our nation," says Health and Human Services Secretary Tommy G. Thompson. "Of course the ulti-

mate cost can't be measured in dollars . . . the ultimate cost to Americans is in chronic disease and early death."

According to the *Annals of Internal Medicine* and the American College of Physicians, adults who were obese at age forty lived six to seven years less than their counterparts of "normal" weight. Adults who were obese and smoked lived thirteen to fourteen years less than people of "normal" weight who didn't smoke. (Each year about 300,000 Americans die prematurely of obesity-related conditions, and 400,000 die of tobacco-related conditions!) The obvious conclusion is that being overweight or obese significantly shortens life expectancy, not to mention quality of life. One report claims that the effects of obesity are like aging twenty years.

Obese adults aren't the only ones who have their lives cut short. According to the Surgeon General of the United States, each year obesity-related conditions kill more American children than gun violence. Wellness International reports that one in four American kids already show weight-linked signs of type 2 diabetes. Sixty percent already have at least one risk factor for heart disease. Where will they be in twenty years?

Protecting Our Most Precious "Commodity"

Being overweight or obese costs. Whether our size limits our lifestyle, the number of friends we have, or the kinds of jobs we can obtain, or it simply impacts our most precious commodity—our health—excess weight hurts us. Furthermore, if the obesity epidemic continues at its current rate, excess body weight will not only kill many of us at a relatively young age, researchers warn that it might overburden and cripple the entire health-care system. Denial won't make its consequences go away. We, as a society, must come to terms with this growing epidemic. How? By first admitting it exists, then deciding the cost is simply too high.

Awareness of the problem is half the battle. By acknowledging that American society is on an unhealthy path, we can begin exploring options for changing our direction. Some of the changes will have to come from individuals in the form of adopting healthy lifestyles, visiting their doctors, and becoming committed to good health. Other changes will have to come from the larger society, perhaps in the form of obesity-prevention programs in our schools, public-awareness campaigns, and improvements to the health-care system. Weight issues will certainly continue to be major challenges to Americans for years to come, but now you are more educated about the realities of America's obesity crisis. With knowledge, you can become part of the solution.

Glossary

accessible: The ability to be reached or attained.

acuity: Keenness of the senses or of intellect.

anatomical: Relating to the physical structure of animals.

autoimmune: Caused by an antibody to substances occurring naturally in the body.

calcifies: Becomes abnormally hard or stiffens due to the deposit of calcium.

carcinomas: Malignant tumors.

catheter: A thin, flexible tube that is inserted into the body to inject or drain fluid.

chronic: A condition that lasts for a long time or recurs frequently.

colorectal: Relating to the colon and rectum.

cultural: Relating to the customary beliefs, social norms, and traits of a racial, religious, ethnic, or social group.

diagnostic: Used in identifying the cause of a disorder.

dialysis: The procedure of filtering accumulated waste products from someone whose kidneys are not functioning correctly.

embolism: A condition in which an artery is blocked by a blood clot.

esophageal: Relating to the passageway down which food moves from the throat to the stomach.

ethnicity: A particular ethnic affiliation or group.

fraternal twins: Twins who develop from two eggs.

free radical: An atom produced naturally in the body or introduced by an outside source that can damage cells, proteins, and DNA by changing their chemical structure.

genetics: Relating to or caused by genes.

gluttonous: Marked by excessive eating or drinking.

hereditary: Transmitted from parent to child by genes.

hypertrophy: An unnatural growth in the size of an organ.

ignorance: Lack of knowledge.

laypeople: Individuals who are not trained in an area.

metabolic: Relating to the total of how a particular substance is handled by a living body.

narcotic: A drug that has effects that range from a mild dulling of the senses, pain relief, and sleep to coma and convulsions.

neurochemical: Relating to the chemical makeup of the nerve tissue.

nonsteroidal anti-inflammatory medications: Drugs that do not use steroids to reduce swelling and relieve pain.

physiological: Relating to the way living creatures function.

postmenopausal: Occurring after menopause, the time in a woman's life when menstruation ceases.

repercussions: Things, especially unforeseen problems, that result from an action.

saturated fats: Fats that come from animals and animal products.

sedentary: Involving much sitting and little exercise.

socioeconomic: Involving economic and social factors.

stethoscope: An instrument through which a health-care practitioner can listen to the heart and lungs.

stroke: A sudden blockage or rupture of a blood vessel in the brain.

trans-fatty acids: Potentially harmful unsaturated fats produced when liquid vegetable oil is made solid through hydrogenation.

visceral: Relating to or affecting a body's internal organs.

Further Reading

Berg, Frances M. *Children and Teens Afraid to Eat*. Hettinger, N.Dak.: Healthy Weight Network, 2001.

Gaesser, Glenn. *Big Fat Lies: The Truth about Your Weight and Your Health*. Carlsbad, Calif.: Gürze Books, 2002.

Gilbert, Sara D. *You Are What You Eat: A Common Sense Guide to the Modern American Diet*. New York: Macmillan, 1997.

Landau, Elaine. *Weight: A Teenage Concern*. New York: Lodestar Books, 1991.

LeBow, Michael D. *Overweight Teenagers: Don't Bear the Burden Alone*. New York: Plenum Press, 1995.

McGraw, Jay. *The Ultimate Weight Solution for Teens*. New York: Simon and Schuster, 2003.

McMillan, Daniel. *Obesity*. New York: Franklin Watts, 1994.

Ojeda, Linda. *Safe Dieting for Teens*. Alameda, Calif.: Hunter House, 1993.

Piscatella, Joseph P. and Barry A. Franklin, *Take a Load off Your Heart*. New York: Workman Publishing Company, 2003.

For More Information

American Dietetic Association
www.eatright.org

Blubber Busters
www.blubberbusters.com

Centers for Disease Control and Prevention
www.cdc.gov

Cool Nurse
www.coolnurse.healthology.com

The Healthy Weight Network
402 South 14th Street
Hettinger, ND 58639
701-567-2646
www.healthyweight.net

National Association to Advance Fat Acceptance
www.naafa.org

National Center for Health Statistics
www.cdc.gov/nchs

The National Institute of Diabetes, Digestive and Kidney Diseases
www.niddk.nih.gov

National Institutes of Health
www.nih.gov

National Library of Medicine
www.nlm.nih.gov

Publisher's note:
The Web sites listed on this page were active at the time of publication. The publisher is not responsible for Web sites that have changed their addresses or discontinued operation since the date of publication. The publisher will review and update the Web site list upon each reprint.

Index

Biographies

Jean Ford is a freelance author, writer, and public speaker. She resides in Perkasie, Pennsylvania, with her husband of twenty-one years, Michael, and their two adolescent children, Kristin and Kyle. She is the author of six books including *Surviving the Roller Coaster: A Teen's Guide to Coping with Moods*, *Right on Schedule! A Teen's Guide to Growth and Development*, and *The Truth about Diets: The Pros and Cons*. Internationally recognized, her work also includes writing for periodicals from the United States to China and speaking to audiences from as close as her tristate area to as far away as Africa. Although she generally writes and speaks on nonfiction topics, Jean also enjoys writing and illustrating children's books.

Dr. Victor F. Garcia is the co-director of the Comprehensive Weight Management Center at Cincinnati Children's Hospital Medical Center. He is a board member of Discover Health of Greater Cincinnati, a fellow of the American College of Surgeons, and a two-time winner of the Martin Luther King Humanitarian Award.

Picture Credits

Banana Stock: pp. 81, 95
Benjamin Stewart: pp. 18, 24, 42, 58, 68, 78, 90
Clipart.com: pp. 15, 21, 22, 36, 60, 67, 72, 98
Dover: p. 10
Hemera Images: pp. 41, 55, 63, 74, 93
Imagesource: pp. 16, 31, 39, 83, 86, 96, 97
MK Bassett-Harvey: p. 6
Photos.com: pp. 18, 19, 28, 30, 37, 45, 50, 53, 77, 88
PhotoDisc: pp. 33, 47, 56
Stockbyte: p. 14

04 06